THE UNIVERSE
BLACK HOLES

ABDO
Publishing Company

A Buddy Book **by Marcia Zappa**

Buddy BOOKS
The Universe

VISIT US AT
www.abdopublishing.com

Published by ABDO Publishing Company, 8000 West 78th Street, Edina, Minnesota 55439.

Printed in the United States of America, North Mankato, Minnesota.
102010
012011

♲ PRINTED ON RECYCLED PAPER

Coordinating Series Editor: Rochelle Baltzer
Contributing Editors: Megan M. Gunderson, BreAnn Rumsch, Sarah Tieck
Graphic Design: Maria Hosley
Cover Photograph: *NASA*: Dana Berry.
Interior Photographs/Illustrations: *AP Photo*: AP Photo (p. 25), NASA/HO (p. 30); *Getty Images*: Time Life Pictures/Mansell (p. 23); *iStockphoto*: ©iStockphoto.com/joshblake (p. 28), ©iStockphoto.com/salihauter (p. 29); *NASA*: CXC/CIA/R.Kraft et al. (p. 19), Dana Berry (p. 9), JPL-Caltech (p. 13), JPL-Caltech/UCLA (p. 15), NASA (pp. 7, 17, 27), X-ray: CXC/MIT/C.Canizares, M.Nowak;Optical: STScl (p. 21); *Photo Researchers, Inc.*: Atlas Photo Bank (p. 14), Viktor Habbick Visions (p. 11); *Shutterstock*: Viktar Malyshchyts (p. 5).

Library of Congress Cataloging-in-Publication Data

Zappa, Marcia, 1985-
  Black holes / Marcia Zappa.
    p. cm. -- (The universe)
  ISBN 978-1-61714-686-2
  1. Black holes (Astronomy)--Juvenile literature. I. Title.
  QB843.B55Z37 2011
  523.8'875--dc22
                              2010028580

Table Of Contents

What Is a Black Hole?

At night, people can see the moon and stars in the sky. Sometimes, they can see planets glowing brightly.

There are also many objects that people can't see in the night sky. Some of these objects are black holes.

Earth and the sun are part of the Milky Way galaxy. Scientists believe the Milky Way contains millions of black holes!

A Closer Look

A black hole is not really a hole. It is an area of space with very strong **gravity**. The pull of gravity is so strong that nothing can escape.

All of a black hole's matter is squeezed into one tiny point. This point is called a singularity. It is at the center of a black hole.

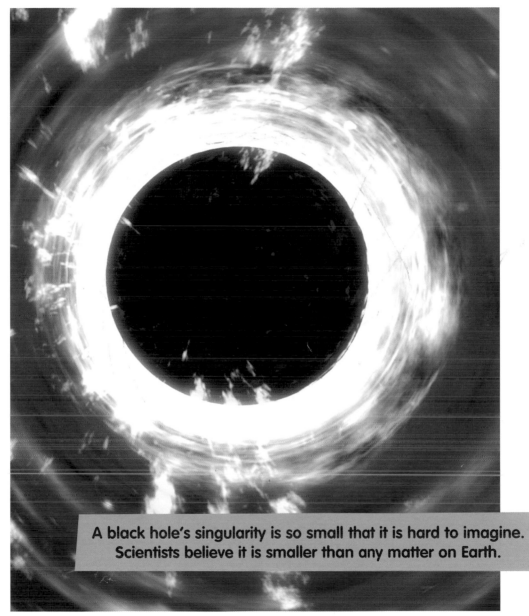

A black hole's singularity is so small that it is hard to imagine.
Scientists believe it is smaller than any matter on Earth.

A black hole's surface is called an event horizon. It is not a surface that you can see or touch. The event horizon is an imaginary **sphere**.

Once an object crosses the event horizon, it cannot escape. It gets quickly pulled into the center of the black hole! There, it becomes part of the black hole's singularity.

Inside the event horizon, objects move faster than the speed of light. Light moves 186,282 miles (299,792 km) per second in space!

Birth of a Black Hole

Black holes form when giant stars burn out. When a star burns **fuel**, it creates a powerful force. This force pushes outward against a star's **gravity**.

After a star runs out of fuel, it can no longer fight its gravity. This causes the star to cave in. A very large star can cave in to a singularity. This forms a black hole.

Black holes grow by pulling in surrounding matter. Scientists believe very large black holes form over billions of years.

Different Sizes

Black holes come in many sizes. Scientists measure the distance from a black hole's center to its event horizon. They use this to find out the black hole's **mass**.

Black holes are measured in solar masses. One solar mass is equal to the mass of our sun.

Almost all black holes fit into two groups. Stellar black holes have just a few solar masses. Supermassive black holes have a million or more solar masses!

Scientists believe most galaxies have a supermassive black hole at the center. They think the Milky Way has a black hole about 4 million times the mass of our sun!

Busy Work

Some black holes are very active. They busily pull in nearby matter. This produces a lot of **energy**.

Some faraway galaxies have bright centers called quasars (KWAY-zahrs). Scientists believe quasars are powered by very large, active black holes.

Other black holes no longer pull in much matter. Scientists call them quiescent (kweye-EH-suhnt).

Many supermassive black holes are quiescent. Scientists believe they are older than active black holes.

The Andromeda galaxy is the closest large galaxy to the Milky Way. At its center is a supermassive quiescent black hole.

Studying the Unseen

Black holes are powerful and mysterious. Not even light can escape the pull of a black hole's **gravity**. This means black holes can't be seen! So, they are very difficult to study.

16

Scientists learn about black holes by looking at nearby matter. They study space objects that **orbit** a black hole. They observe the speed and size of the objects. This tells them how big the black hole is.

Sometimes a black hole and a star closely orbit each other. This is called a binary system.

Scientists also study dust, gas, and space objects being pulled toward a black hole. When matter is pulled by a black hole's **gravity**, it speeds up.

This creates **energy** that gives off light. Some of the light is in forms that the human eye cannot see. These include X-ray and radio waves. Scientists use special **telescopes** to study this light.

Light travels in wavelike patterns. X-ray waves are much shorter than the visible light humans can see. Radio waves are much longer.

X-ray Waves

Visible Light

Radio Waves

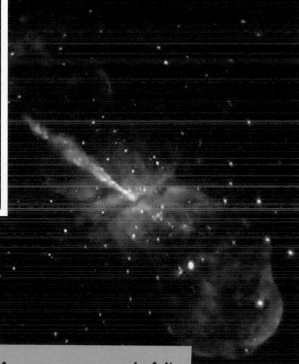

Many pictures of space are very colorful! That is because they show X-ray waves, visible light, and radio waves.

Crash Course

Some galaxies have more than one black hole. Scientists expect that someday two black holes may hit.

If two black holes hit, they would join together. They would form one big black hole! This would be a very powerful event.

Scientists do not know exactly what would happen if black holes crashed. But, they believe it would create huge amounts of **energy** called gravitational waves. Gravitational waves affect time and space.

Black Hole   Black Hole

The two black holes in the NGC 6240 galaxy are only 3,000 light-years apart. Scientists believe they could join together in tens to hundreds of millions of years.

Discovering Black Holes

Scientists first suggested the idea of black holes in the late 1700s. English scientist John Michell printed his ideas in 1783. In 1795, French scientist Pierre-Simon Laplace printed his ideas.

Michell and Laplace came up with their **theories** separately. But, they both based them on what they knew about **gravity**.

Pierre-Simon Laplace

Current facts about black holes are based on Albert Einstein's ideas. In 1916, Einstein printed the general **theory** of relativity. This theory explained how **gravity** changes time, light, and space.

Around 1967, American scientist John Archibald Wheeler first used the name *black hole*. He also led many important studies about black holes.

Albert Einstein was a famous
scientist. He was born in Germany
and later became a U.S. citizen.

Exploring Black Holes

Today, scientists use powerful **telescopes** to study black holes. Some telescopes are on Earth. Others are in space.

In 1999, **NASA** sent the Chandra X-ray Observatory into space. This telescope gives scientists data from X-rays. This helps them locate black holes.

The Hubble Space Telescope was sent into orbit in 1990. It has taken pictures of some of the farthest space objects ever seen.

Fact Trek

A black hole's strong **gravity** has odd effects on its nearby area. Scientists believe it can slow time and bend light beams.

Some black holes spin around a straight line called an axis.

Many stars and planets such as Earth also spin around an axis.

Our sun is not big enough to become a black hole. A star needs to be at least three times bigger than the sun to become a black hole.

The sun may seem huge. But, it is only a medium-sized star.

The closest black hole to Earth is about 1,600 light-years away. One light-year is nearly 6 trillion miles (10 trillion km)! So, there is no real danger of Earth being pulled into a black hole.

Voyage to Tomorrow

People continue to use new ways to study black holes. Recently, scientists created large tools to measure gravitational waves from Earth.

Scientists hope to send this type of tool into space! A **mission** called LISA is creating a spacecraft for this purpose. Scientists hope LISA will find new facts about black holes.

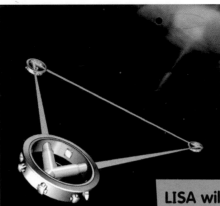

LISA will orbit our sun. It will have three spacecraft connected by laser beams.

Important Words

energy usable power. Heat is one form of energy.

fuel (FYOOL) something burned to give heat or power.

gravity a natural force that pulls toward the center of a space object. It also pulls space objects toward each other.

mass an amount of matter.

mission the sending of spacecraft to do certain jobs.

NASA National Aeronautics and Space Administration. NASA is run by the U.S. government to study Earth, our solar system, and outer space.

orbit the path of a space object as it moves around another space object. To orbit is to follow this path.

sphere (SFIHR) a ball-shaped object.

telescope a tool used for viewing faraway objects, such as stars.

theory an explanation of how or why something happens.

Web Sites

To learn more about **black holes**, visit ABDO Publishing Company online. Web sites about **black holes** are featured on our Book Links page. These links are routinely monitored and updated to provide the most current information available.

www.abdopublishing.com

INDEX